Now we
know about...

HEALTHY EATING

Deborah Chancellor
Crabtree Publishing Company
www.crabtreebooks.com

Published in Canada
Crabtree Publishing
616 Welland Avenue,
St. Catharines, Ontario
L2M 5V6

Published in the United States
Crabtree Publishing
PMB 16A,
350 Fifth Avenue, Suite 3308
New York, NY 10118

Editors: Belinda Weber, Lynn Peppas, Reagan Miller
Editorial director: Kathy Middleton
Production coordinator: Kenneth Wright
Prepress technician: Kenneth Wright
Studio manager: Sara Greasley
Designer: Trudi Webb
Production controller: Ed Green
Production manager: Suzy Kelly

Picture credits:
iStock: p. 10 (right), 12, 22 (bottom left)
Shutterstock: front cover, back cover (center right), p. 1, 4, 5, 6, 7, 8–9,
    10 (left), 11, 13, 14, 15, 16–17, 18, 19, 20, 21, 22 (bottom right), 23

Every effort has been made to trace copyright holders, and we apologize in
advance for any omissions. We would be pleased to insert the appropriate
acknowledgments in any subsequent edition of this publication.

Library and Archives Canada Cataloguing in Publication

Chancellor, Deborah
   Healthy eating / Deborah Chancellor.

(Now we know about)
Includes index.
ISBN 978-0-7787-4720-8 (bound).--ISBN 978-0-7787-4737-6 (pbk.)

      1. Nutrition--Juvenile literature. I. Title.
II. Series: Now we know about (St. Catharines, Ont.)

RA784.C44 2009   j613.2   C2009-903118-3

Library of Congress Cataloging-in-Publication Data

Chancellor, Deborah.
   Healthy eating / Deborah Chancellor.
      p. cm. -- (Now we know about)
   Includes index.
   ISBN 978-0-7787-4737-6 (pbk. : alk. paper) -- ISBN 978-0-
7787-4720-8 (reinforced library binding : alk. paper)
      1. Nutrition--Juvenile literature. I. Title.

RA784.C444 2010
613.2--dc22

                                        2009020919

Contents

Fabulous food

Do you wonder why you get hungry? Hunger is your body's way of letting you know it needs healthy foods. Healthy means it is good for you.

Healthy food keeps your body working at its best.

Why do you eat?

Food gives you energy. You need energy to play, to learn, and to grow. Your body even needs energy when you sleep!

mixed vegetables

What are calories?

Some kinds of foods give you a lot of energy. The energy in food is **measured** in **calories**. Food that is high in energy has a lot of calories.

How are you feeling?

You need to eat healthy foods to stay well. Eating too much of the wrong kinds of food can make you sick.

Talking Point

Why should you try to eat healthy food?

Fresh food is good for you. When food is fresh it is raw, or not cooked. Fresh food is food that is not frozen. It does not come in a can, or jar. Fresh food has the **vitamins** and **minerals** you need. Try to eat as much fresh food as you can.

If you are not well, eating healthy foods will help you get better.

Children need to eat healthy foods to grow.

5

Eat your five-a-day

You need to eat five portions of fruits and vegetables a day. A portion is a piece of fruit, one serving of a vegetable, or a fruit juice drink.

Vitamins and minerals help you grow.

What are vitamins and minerals?

Vitamins and minerals are nutrients found in fruits and vegetables. Vitamins and minerals help keep you fit and well.

WORD WIZARD!

nutrient

A nutrient is a natural chemical in food. Nutrients help you grow and stay healthy

What is fiber?

Some food is hard to **digest**. This means it takes a while to pass through your body. **Fiber** is a nutrient that helps you digest. Fiber is found in many fruits and leafy vegetables.

Talking Point

What should you do if you do not like fruits or vegetables?

Try to drink fruit juice. A drink of pure fruit juice counts as one portion of fruit. There are many delicious fruits and vegetables. Do not be afraid to try new ones. You may find some you enjoy!

Fruits and vegetables contain fiber.

Food for life

You need energy to get fit and keep your body healthy. High-energy foods help you stay moving for a long time.

Playing sports uses up energy, which makes you hungry. You need to eat to get your strength back.

What are carbohydrates?

Carbohydrates are foods that give you a lot of energy. They are very filling. They stop you from feeling hungry again for a while.

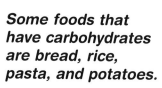

Some foods that have carbohydrates are bread, rice, pasta, and potatoes.

What are pulses?

Pulses are seeds that grow inside plant pods. Beans and lentils are pulses. Pulses add **protein** to your **diet**.

pulses

whole-grain bread

Eat whole-grain foods. When you eat a sandwich use whole-grain bread instead of white bread.

What are whole grains?

Try to eat whole grains in your diet, such as wheat, barley, and oats. Whole grains are natural. They are not made in a factory. Whole grains are a good way to get fiber, vitamins, and protein.

9

Do you drink milk?

Dairy foods come from farm animals that make milk. Cows and goats give milk. Cheese and yogurt are made from milk. They are dairy foods, too.

What is the other choice?

Some people do not want to eat dairy foods. Others cannot eat dairy foods because they are allergic to them. Some people choose non-dairy foods, such as soy milk, instead of dairy foods.

Dairy foods contain a nutrient called calcium. *Calcium is good for your bones and teeth.*

cow's milk

soy milk

Some people like to drink soy milk. Soy comes from vegetables.

Are eggs dairy food?

Eggs are not a dairy food. They are not a meat either. They have a nutrient called protein. Protein helps make your muscles and bones grow.

Free-range chickens are farmed in a natural way. They can go outside to find food.

WORD WIZARD!

allergic
If you are allergic to something, you have a sensitive reaction to it

Talking Point

Why are dairy foods good for you?

Dairy foods give you calcium. Calcium helps your teeth and bones grow and stay strong. Children need to get more calcium than adults. This is because their bodies are still growing.

eggs

11

Eating meat

Meat has protein. Protein is good for you. It helps you grow. It helps your body get better if you are hurt.

Meat can be an important part of a healthy diet.

steak with vegetables

What kinds of meat are there?

Beef and lamb are red meats. Chicken and pork are white meats. Most fast-food meals have processed meat. This is made from meat but has other foods added to it too.

Do you like meat?

A small amount of meat is good for you. But do not eat too much every day. Many stores sell other choices for meat, such as soy or tofu.

Many burgers contain meat, but they are also full of fat and salt.

What is a vegetarian?

Vegetarians do not eat meat. They get all their nutrients from vegetables and vegetable products, such as tofu and soy.

Some vegetarians do not like that animals are killed for their meat.

Talking Point

What is a vegan?

Vegans are vegetarians who do not eat animal products. They do not eat eggs or cheese. They do not drink milk. Many vegans do not wear wool, or eat honey because it is made from animals. They get all their nutrients from vegetables.

Do you eat fish?

It is a good idea to eat fish two times a week. One of your fish meals should include an oily fish. Mackerel, salmon, and sardines are oily fish. Oily fish are full of healthy nutrients.

Oily fish contains vitamins that are good for your eyes, skin, hair, bones, and teeth.

salmon

Why choose fish?

Eating fish adds protein to your diet. Fish also have a lot of minerals. Fish is not as fattening as some meats, such as pork or lamb.

fresh fish

Which fish is best?

The oil in oily fish is called "unsaturated" **fat**. Fish oil has a nutrient called "Omega 3." Omega 3 helps your heart stay healthy. It also helps different parts of your body work well, such as your brain.

Eating oily fish is good for your brain. It can help you focus on your work.

Talking Point

Why is fish good for you?

Fish is full of healthy vitamins, minerals, and protein. It has a healthy kind of fat. It is good for your heart and brain.

WORD WIZARD!

unsaturated fat
This kind of fat is liquid at room temperature. Unsaturated fat can be good for your heart.

What are fatty foods?

You do not need much fat in your diet. The two kinds of fat are saturated and unsaturated fats. Unsaturated fats are better for you than saturated fats.

What should I eat?

Try to eat foods that are made with unsaturated fats. For a snack, try nuts instead of potato chips.

donut

Donuts contain saturated fat. They should only be eaten as a treat.

Nuts and olive oil have unsaturated fats.

Cookies, cakes, and chocolate contain saturated fats.

Sweet potatoes have more nutrients than other kinds of potatoes.

sweet potatoes

Talking Point

Why should you try not to eat fatty snacks?

Snacks that are full of saturated fats are bad for your heart. Fatty snacks can make you put on weight. Choose a healthy snack instead, such as a piece of fruit.

Is it fattening?

Fatty foods give you energy. But they can make you gain weight if you eat too much of them. Starchy foods, such as potatoes, fruits, and vegetables are also high in energy. They are much less fattening.

17

Snack attack

Sugar and salt make food taste better. But you do not need a lot of sugar and salt in your diet. Too much sugar will rot your teeth. Too much salt is bad for your health.

Many snacks contain sugar or salt.

salty snacks

Avoid tooth decay

Try not to eat too many sugary foods and drinks. Sugar left in your mouth turns into a sticky substance called plaque. Plaque can cause **tooth decay.**

Brush your teeth about one hour after you eat sweets.

Does it need salt?

Many **convenience foods** are very salty. You do not need that extra salt. A salty diet is bad for your heart.

French fries are a type of convenience food.

Talking point

Why do food companies add salt to their products?

Salt is a good way to make food last a long time. Long ago it was used to keep food from going bad. Salt also adds flavor to some foods.

Make a choice

Snacks do not have to be sweet or salty. Try eating healthy snacks next time you are hungry. Eat fruits, plain popcorn, unsalted peanuts, or breadsticks, instead.

fruit

breadsticks

19

Drink up

You need to eat and drink to stay healthy. More than half of your body is made up of water!

Try to drink at least four to eight cups (one to two liters) a day. Do not drink too many sugary drinks.

It is good to drink water throughout the day. Do not wait until you feel thirsty.

glass of water

Are you thirsty?

When you **exercise** you sweat. Your body loses water. This makes you thirsty. You also sweat when you are hot. You should drink more water on warm summer days.

How does your body tell you that you need a drink?

When your body needs liquid your mouth gets dry. You feel thirsty. You need to drink some water to replace the liquid your body has used.

watermelon

Can you eat water?

About half of the water you get comes from the foods you eat. Fruits and vegetables are foods that contain water. You get the rest of your water by drinking.

What is a balanced diet?

You should eat three balanced meals a day. In between meals you can have one or two healthy snacks. Remember to eat foods from each of the different food groups.

This picture shows how much of each food group you should eat. Eat a lot of fruits and vegetables. Do not eat very many fats or sugars.

apple

Bread, cereals, and potatoes

Milk, cheese, and yogurt

Fats and sugar

Meat, fish, and eggs

Fruits and vegetables

Have you had enough?

It is important to eat the right kinds of foods. It is also important to eat the right amount. If you eat too much, or too little, you can get sick.

Hindus believe that cows are holy animals.

Off the menu?

Some people do not eat some kinds of foods for religious reasons. Jewish people do not eat pork. Hindus do not eat beef.

Talking Point

Why is it important to eat a balanced diet?

A **balanced diet** gives you the different nutrients you need to stay healthy. Eat a lot of different kinds of foods. Eat from each of the food groups. Do not be afraid to try new foods.

Are you hungry?

Do not fill up on fatty snacks between meals. Try high fiber snacks instead. Foods with fiber stop you from feeling hungry because they take a long time to digest.

23

Glossary

balanced diet The foods you eat that have all the nutrients you need to be healthy

calcium A mineral found in some foods, which is good for bones and teeth

calorie A way to measure the amount of energy in food

carbohydrate Important foods that give you a lot of energy

convenience food Ready-made foods that can be made quickly

dairy food Foods that comes from farm animals that can be milked

diet The foods that you usually eat

digest To break down food so that nutrients can be taken from it

exercise Doing things that keep you moving so you get strong and stay healthy

fat A part of food that gives you energy. Eating too much fat can make you gain weight

fiber A nutrient in some foods that helps you digest

measure To find out the size, or how many of something

mineral A nutrient in foods that is good for you

protein A nutrient in foods that helps you grow and be strong

tooth decay Damage to a tooth caused by eating sweet foods and poor brushing habits

vegetarian Someone who does not eat meat, meat products, or fish

vitamin A nutrient found in foods that helps you grow and stay healthy

Index

Printed In the U.S.A.- CG